WILD CATS

Lions

Anne Welsbacher
ABDO Publishing Company

visit us at
www.abdopub.com

Published by Abdo Publishing Company 4940 Viking Drive, Edina, Minnesota 55435. Copyright © 2000 by Abdo Consulting Group, Inc. International copyrights reserved in all countries. No part of this book may be reproduced in any form without written permission from the publisher.

Printed in the United States.

Photo credits: Peter Arnold, Inc.

Edited by Lori Kinstad Pupeza
Contributing editor Morgan Hughes

Library of Congress Cataloging-in-Publication Data

Welsbacher, Anne, 1955-
    Lions / Anne Welsbacher.
    p. cm. -- (Wild cats)
    Includes index.
    Summary: Describes the physical characteristics, social, feeding, and hunting behavior, and life cycle of this big cat.
    ISBN 1-57765-086-7
    1. Lions--Juvenile literature. [1. Lions.] I. Title. II. Series: Welsbacher, Anne, 1955- Wild cats.
    QL737.C23W45   2000
    599.757--dc21   98-4554
                                                                 CIP
                                                                 AC

Contents

Wild Cats around the World

*T*he lion is one kind of wild cat. Lions live in Africa. A small number of lions live in India. Other wild cats live in South America, Asia, and Mexico. Some places, like Antarctica, have no wild cats at all.

All wild cats are good hunters. They have sharp claws and teeth. They pounce on animals, catch them, and eat them.

Each kind of wild cat has something special. Lions have big furry **manes**. No other cats have manes. A mane is made of long, thick hair that grows around a lion's neck and head.

Lions also roar. No wild cat roars as loud as the lion! That is why lions sometimes are called the king of beasts.

A young lion in Kenya, Africa.

Big Cat, Little Cat

Wild cats are like house cats in many ways. House cats like to hunt, just like their bigger cousins. They also have sharp claws. And most big and little cats can pull their claws into their paws—or stretch them out to scratch.

Both wild cats and tame cats have whiskers. Both can see very well at night. Both lick themselves to keep clean.

Most wild cats like to be alone, but lions are **social**. This means they like to live with other lions.

Many house cats are social, too. They like to live with people!

Most wild cats roar. But house cats do not roar. They purr. Lions can do both!

House cats lie with their tails curled up close. But most wild cats stretch their tails out long. The lion has something extra—a puff of fur at the tip of its tail!

Lions like to be with other lions. A group of lions is called a pride.

A Closer Look

Lions are 8 to 10 feet (2 to 3 m) long, counting their tails. That is almost as long as two children lying end to end!

A male lion can weigh 400 to 500 pounds (182 to 227 kg), about the same as eight or nine small kids! Female lions weigh 250 to 350 pounds (113 to 159 kilograms).

The lion has golden brown fur. Its fur blends in with the land and grass where the lion lives. This makes it harder for others to see the lion.

Male lions have **manes**. Females do not. The mane on a young lion is light brown. It turns to dark brown or black as the lion gets older.

Lions have very big eyes, bigger than the eyes of any other wild cats. They can see very well at night.

A lion has strong shoulders and front legs. It has big paws and long claws. It also has four big teeth that hang long, like fangs. These are called **canine** teeth.

A male lion with a large mane.

The Lion at Home

*L*ions live in flat, open grasslands with only a few trees and bushes. They like very hot, dry weather. The area and climate lions live in is called their **habitat**.

Lions live in the south and east parts of Africa. They also live in one small part of India.

Long ago, there were a large number of lions in many countries. They lived in Europe, the Middle East, Asia, and Africa. But most of them were hunted and killed.

Today most lions live in special parks that keep them safe. These parks are called **preserves**.

Three lions drinking water in a wildlife preserve in Africa.

A Champion Roar

*T*he place where certain lions live is called their
territory. A lion's territory can be 15 to 150 square miles (39
to 388 sq km). Lions roar to keep out other animals. The
roar also helps other lions find each other. You can hear a
lion's roar five miles (eight km) away.

Lions are lazy. They sleep or rest 17 to 20 hours a day!
They hunt at night. When they get thirsty, lions scoop water
into their mouths with their tongues. It takes about 10
minutes for a lion to drink all the water it needs. Lions can
go two or three days without water.

Male lions eat 15 pounds (7 kg) or more of food each
day. Females eat around 11 pounds (5 kg). Some days they
must go without any food. When they finally do eat, they
might eat as much as 75 pounds (34 kg). That is about the
weight of a big desk!

A lion has a powerful roar.

The Predator's Prey

*L*ions are carnivores. A carnivore is an animal that eats meat. They also are called **predators**. The animals they eat are called **prey**.

Lions eat zebras, antelopes, wildebeests, gazelles, wild pigs, and warthogs. These animals all have hooves. They run fast but do not have claws to protect themselves.

Lions can run about 35 miles per hour (56 kmph). But they cannot run for a long time without resting. So lions get as close as they can to animals before they start to chase them.

Female lions do the hunting. They get close to a **herd**, or group, of animals. They spring forward with their strong back legs. They pull down an animal with their strong front legs.

They hold down the animal with their claws. They kill it by biting its neck with their long **canine** teeth.

The males eat first. Then the females. The baby lions, called cubs, eat last.

14

A female lion attacking a wildebeest.

Cat to Cat

*L*ions like to be with other lions. They live in groups called prides. A lion pride can have from 4 to 35 or more lions in it. The lions take turns being the leader of the pride.

A pride has two or more female lions, their cubs, and two or more males. The female lions take care of the cubs and do most of the hunting. They roar softly to call their cubs.

The male lions take care of their **territory**. They walk all around it to make sure no other animals enter. If they do, the lions scare them away with a big roar! They also roar every day before sunrise and after sunset.

Lions walk with their tails held high in the air. Their cubs can see them above the grass. The tail also warns outside lions to stay away.

Lions rub against each other or lick each other to say hello. They growl before they get into a fight. And they purr when they are happy!

Cubs playing with a female lion.

Cat Families

When a female lion is three to four years old, she chooses a male lion. They leave the pride for a few days to **mate**.

Then they return to the pride. The female finds a **den**. Here she can give birth and keep her cubs hidden and safe.

After three and a half months, the female gives birth to two to four cubs. They are about as long as a person's arm. They weigh three to four pounds (one to two kg).

The cubs are born with their eyes closed. They cannot walk. They have spots, called **rosettes**. Later the spots will go away.

They do not yet have **manes**. Later, the male cubs will grow sandy-colored manes. The manes will get thicker and darker as they grow.

The newborn cubs **nurse** their mother. Soon she must go back to hunting. One female lion stays with all the cubs to protect them from **predators**.

Lion cubs.

Growing Up

*A*fter two weeks, the cubs' eyes open. In six weeks, they can walk. Now they can leave their **dens** and start to explore.

The cubs practice hunting by chasing each other. They even chase the tails of their father or other male lions.

At three months, the cubs join hunting trips. For the first time, they eat meat. By the time the cubs are one and a half years, they can hunt by themselves. By the time they are two, they are young adult lions.

When female lions are three or four, they can have their own cubs. Male lions leave their pride at that age. They are driven from the pride and often leave in a group to form their own pride. Others become **nomads**, lions that are alone. The nomads try to find another pride to join.

By age five, a lion is full grown. The male's **mane** is thick, long, and dark. The lion can live to be 20 years old.

A full-grown male lion.

21

Glossary

Canines—long, fanglike teeth that help kill prey.

Den—a safe place made of rocks, bushes, or other things, where animals live and have babies.

Habitat—the area and climate that an animal lives in.

Herd—a group of animals.

Mane—a bunch of long, thick hair that grows around a lion's neck and head. The mane helps protect the lion in fights.

Mate—to join in a pair in order to produce young.

Nomad—a lone lion that does not live in a pride.

Nurse—lion cubs getting milk from their mother.

Predator—an animal that eats other animals.

Preserve—a special park where wild animals can live safe from hunting and other human activities.

Prey—an animal that is eaten by other animals.

Rosette—a black spot or circle on a lion cub.

Social—a person or animal that likes to be with other people or animals.

Territory—an area or place where certain animals live; if others enter this area, the animal might fight or scare them off.

Internet Sites

Tiger Information Center
http://www.5tigers.org/
The Tiger Information Center is dedicated to providing information to help preserve the remaining five subspecies of tigers. This is a great site, with many links, sound, and animation.

The Lion Research Center
http://www.lionresearch.org/
Everything you want to know about lions is here. Lion research and conservation in Africa, information on lion behavior, and updates from researchers in the Serengeti about specific lion prides.

The Cheetah Spot
http://ThingsWild.com/cheetah2.html
This is a cool spot with sound and animation. Lots of fun information.

Amur Leopard
http://www.scz.org/asian/amurl1.html
This site links you to some great zoo spots. Very informative.

These sites are subject to change. Go to your favorite search engine and type in "cats" for more sites.

PASS IT ON

Tell Others What You Like About Animals!

To educate readers around the country, pass on interesting tips about animals, maybe a fun story about your animal or pet, and little-known facts about animals. We want to hear from you!

To get posted on the ABDO Publishing Company Web site, email us at "animals@abdopub.com"

Visit us at www.abdopub.com

Index